# CAPTIVATED

# CULTIVATED

# COMMISSIONED

Growing in your relationship with Jesus by becoming captivated by who he is, cultivated by what he thought, and commissioned with the mission he gave.

## DREW ALAN HALL

Published by KHARIS PUBLISHING, an imprint of KHARIS MEDIA LLC.

Copyright © 2025 Drew Alan Hall
ISBN-13: 978-1-63746-658-2
ISBN-10: 1-63746-658-7
Library of Congress Control Number:

All KHARIS PUBLISHING products are available at special quantity discounts for bulk purchases for sales promotions, premiums, fund-raising, and educational needs. For details, contact:
Kharis Media LLC
Tel: +1 (331) 312-2376
support@kharispublishing.com
www.kharispublishing.com

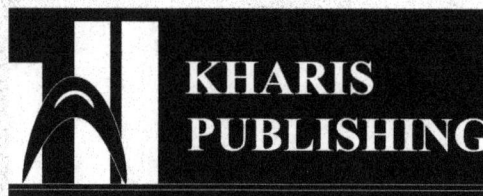

KHARIS
PUBLISHING

# FOREWORD

During my time as a coach, I've been a part of many teams. Each group was different, but they were all searching for some sort of success. As young athletes, they are faced with the challenges of game time pressure, time management, and most importantly, identity once sports end. The grueling truth is that no amount of success on the field can prepare you for the most important question we will all face at some point when we meet Jesus. Our goal as a staff is to help guide these athletes in a direction that allows them to grow as people both on and off the field. This study will allow our team to dig deep into who they are and what their mission is beyond the field of play. Whether it be a sports team or a small group, there is power in hearing someone's heart and seeing how God is moving and using them. We look forward to growing as a team by digging deeper into who Jesus was and by trying to replicate his love each day.

Drew Alan Hall has been a key piece in our overall culture and direction of our program. While sports foster the opportunity to learn many lessons, we've seen the Lord use moments to move our team and grow our hearts to love like His. Drew has poured into the team, myself, and all those around him as if loving others is a habit for him. We are thankful for his mission and his guidance over our program!

**Megan Curry**
**Samford University Softball Coach**

Jesus' final words before His ascension beckon us to "Go and make disciples" (Matt. 28:19-20). This command of Jesus sounds intimidating: "of all nations." How can we embark on such a monumental task? The answer is found at the end of the command– "I am with you always, to the end of the age." Jesus is with us! The presence of the One who created the world and defeated the grave is with us! So, His mission for us is a matter of obedience. Will we go? Will we make disciples? Will we trust that He is with us?

Drew Hall answered these questions with a resounding "Yes!" His passion for sharing the Gospel and making disciples has provided him with many opportunities to preach the Gospel to people of all ages in many different areas. As his pastor, I have been blessed to watch God use him to minister to students and call the church to live out our faith with authenticity.

This book guides disciple-makers in their pursuit of fulfilling the Great Commission. As we learn about Christ, we become more Christ-like. The Holy Spirit sanctifies believers through spiritual disciplines. Scriptures tell us that we discipline ourselves for the purpose of godliness (1 Tim. 4:7) and become doers of the Word, and not hearers only (James1:22). Drew's book encourages us not to treat the Bible as an academic resource, but to consider it as a vital part of one's spiritual walk with Jesus. It is not spiritual homework; it is meant to help you grow closer to Jesus.

It is my prayer that God use Drew Hall's book to challenge believers to take the task of the Great Commission seriously. Remember it is not an option or recommendation. Jesus commanded us to make disciples. When Jesus-followers become disciple- makers, we can make a greater impact on this world for the Kingdom of Christ.

**Dr Ryan Morris**
**Pastor FBC Hokes Bluff**

# FOLLOW ME

The same command and promised outcome Jesus gave Peter and his brother Andrew beside the Sea of Galilee is given to us today. The command comes first: "Follow me," followed by the promise of becoming something different: "I will make you fish for men." The response Jesus wants from us is the response we see in Matthew 4:20, "At once they left their nets and followed Him."This study is not about following Jesus because it is "what you should do". This study is about falling in love with who he is. Learning to be like him and to complete the mission he gave us is the only suitable response after having a radical encounter with the risen Savior.

To help you accomplish that outcome, I have divided this study into three parts. The first falls under the header of being **CAPTIVATED**. We will look at who Jesus is through his own words. As you learn more about Jesus, he will gain more attention and interest in your life. Attention and interest in Jesus never return void. Your life will change, and the change that happens will be for the better. The best version of you is the version that is captivated by Jesus.

The second part of this study focuses on **CULTIVATING** your life with Jesus' teachings. You would never put a trailer hitch on a Ferrari (even if you're from Alabama).Yes, a Ferrari has the power to pull a trailer, but it was not made to pull things. The same is true for our new life in Christ. Trying to do things in your new life that you were not made to do would make no sense. We learn about how to live like Jesus through his teaching and by seeing how he lived. The bible also states in 1$^{st}$ John 2:6 that if we claim to live in him, we must live as he did.

The third part of this study focuses on understanding the **COMMISSION** Jesus gives us. A commission is an instruction, command, or order from an authority figure to an individual or group. There is no higher authority for you and me than Jesus. One great thing about Jesus is that he does not leave us in the dark about the purpose of our lives. People often ask, "What does God want me to do?" In part three, we will engage with that question. Now, a disclaimer from the beginning: I am not promising that through this study, you will figure out exactly what God wants you to do with your life but I promise that you will see how he wants you to do things and why his glory should be the driving force behind the why of your what.

There is no secret sauce to help you follow Jesus. It takes sacrifice, hard work, and, most importantly, the resolve not to quit when things get hard. These are not qualities that I pulled out of thin air. I see these three qualities in Jesus telling the disciples the cost of following him in Matthew 16:24-25: " 24 Then Jesus said to his disciples, 'Whoever wants to be my disciple must deny themselves and take up their cross and followme.25 For whoever wants to save their life will lose it, but whoever loses their life for me will find it". My goal for this study is that you will see that what you gain by following Jesus is far greater than what it costs. I also hope that through this and the community with your group, your faith will be encouraged and inspired to follow hard after Jesus.

# HOW TO USE THIS STUDY

### Planning

To get the most out of any Bible study, one must sacrifice time and attention from other things and put them toward Jesus. Time and sacrifice are two principles that any good relationship is built on. Try to plan out each week. Look at what you have coming up, and go ahead and schedule when you are going to spend time with God. This will also be a helpful habit to help you have consistent time with God after completing this study.

### Community

Life is better in a community. While your relationship with Jesus is personal, it was never meant to be lived out in isolation. During this study, I will ask you to do some things that might be outside of your comfort zone. Not only is the group time necessary, but each week you will get a partner (preferably a different one each week) to be your swim buddy. Navy SEALS use the swim buddy system during training and missions. The rule is you never leave your swim buddy. Going forth with this study, I will ask you to text and talk to your partner daily. Ask them how you can pray for them. Know when they scheduled their time with God and encourage them before or after it. Tell them things you got out of the daily devotions. Accountability is always helpful!

### Memorize

One of my college friends always said, in life, you are either going into a storm or coming out of one. A simple rule that can help you through those times is this: 'Failure to plan is planning to fail. The best way to prepare for the storms of life is to hide God's word in your heart. When Jesus was tempted in the wilderness, he used scripture to rebuke the devil. Each week, we will have a verse to memorize. By creating this habit, hopefully by the end of the year, you would have memorized 52 different bible verses. That's a lot of ammo to help you combat the storms of life.

## Daily Devotions

Studying the bible can be a daunting task. First, it is a big book made up of 66 smaller books. Secondly, the wording can be tricky to understand depending on the translation. Third, people struggle with where even to start studying the bible. The main thing to remember is that the bible is all about the story of God's love and grace and redemption of his people from the consequences of sin. Through this study, you will have the opportunity every day to dive into God's word and practice some skills to help you understand and apply it in the everyday rhythms of life. Read the devotion first, and then spend times studying that day's scripture passage.

## Progress

The last thing to help you during this study is focusing on progress over perfection. In church, we use the term sanctification. That big word means looking more like Jesus and less like the old you. If you are a perfectionist, this may be hard for you. The truth is that we won't be perfect until Jesus comes back and makes everything right. So, on this side of heaven, the focus should be on progress, not perfection. Sometimes progress means that you cuss less today than you did yesterday. Whatever progress looks like for you, celebrate it!

# HOW TO STUDY THE BIBLE

## 1 OBSERVE

- What Do I See
- What Is The Author Saying

## 2 INTERPERATION

- What Does The Author **Mean** By What the Author Is **Saying**
- Is There A Timeless Truth Rising Out Of The Text

## 3 APPLICATION

- How Do I Apply The Timeless Truth
- What Does It Mean For Me In My Life?

A great resource for learning how to study the bible using this method is " Living By The Book" by Howard and William Hendricks

# HOW TO PRAY
# A.C.T.S METHOD

## ADORATION

- Praising God for who he is ( His character, greatness, love, ect.)

## CONFESSION

- Confessing sin in your life and asking for forgivness

## THANKSGIVING

- Thanking God for what he has blessed you with

## SUPPLICATION

- Bringing your request to God for you and others

# SWIMM BUDDY SOP
## ( STANDARD OPERATION PROCEDURE)

### 1 INPUT

- What am I feeding my soul with?
- What TV are you watching, music/ podcast you are listening to, book you are reading?
- Where are you at in the bible?

### 2 OUTPUT

- How have I treated others?
- Who have you shared Jesus with?
- Who have you prayed for?

### 3 CONFESSION

- I was this way with others _____
- I looked at this _____
- I did this _____

These are the questions to ask your partner for the week every day in person or via text. These came from the Be Coming Something podcast.

# TESTIMONY

Week 1

A W TOZER

"WHAT COMES INTO OUR MINDS WHEN WE THINK ABOUT GOD IS THE MOST IMPORTANT THING ABOUT US."

1st Peter 3:15 16 *"15 But in your hearts revere Christ as Lord. Always be prepared to give an answer to everyone who asks you to give the reason for the hope that you have. But do this with gentleness and respect, 16 keeping a clear conscience, so that those who speak maliciously against your good behavior in Christ may be ashamed of their slander."*

Your testimony is simply the story of what happened between you and God. It can be broken down into three parts: the first is what your life was like before Jesus; the second is how you accepted Jesus and ultimately surrendered to him as Lord and Savior; and the third is how your life is different now that you have new life in Jesus. At the end of this session, you will get the chance to write out your testimony.

For our daily devotions this week, we will examine different people's testimonies recorded in the Bible. During this time, look at the three parts in each story. The person's life before Jesus, their encounter with Jesus, and their life after Jesus. One constant thing that you will see in each story is that it was an interaction with Jesus that caused the change. The same is true for us. The catalyst for a radical change in our lives is Jesus.

Before we write out our testimony, we need to make sure we have a testimony about Jesus. That is what the first group session will be centered around. Not only will the questions we look at help you, but they can also be a tool to help you share your faith with others. To testify is to give evidence about something as a witness who experienced it. Why would we not want to share the great testimony that ever happened to us with others? Also, if you love or care about someone, do you not want to make sure they put their faith in the way, the truth, and the life? Learning how to tell your story is also learning how to witness to others about Jesus.

# Important Questions

**QUESTION 01**

On a scale of 1-10, with 1 being not sure at all and 10 being 100% sure, if you dided today how sure are you that you would go to heaven?

1    2    3    4    5    6    7    8    9    10

**QUESTION 02**

If you stood before God today and he asked you why he should let you into heaven what would you say?

**QUESTION 03**

What is Sin?

**QUESTION 04**

What is the conquences of sin?

# THE WORDS OF SALVATION

**DEPRAVITY**
- All Are Sinners

**WRATH**
- The Judgement Of A HOLY GOD AGAINST ALL SIN

**LOVE**
- GOD HAS MERCY ON HIS PEOPLE

**ATONEMENT**
- JESUS DIES AS A PAYMENT FOR ALL SIN

**FORGIVNESS**
- OUR DEBT IS CANCELED BY THE SACRIFICE OF JESUS

**JUSTIFICATION**
- CHRIST RIGHTEOUSNESS IS TRANSFERRED TO US

**SANCTIFICATION**
- SALVATION IS A PROCESS THAT TRANSFORMS OUR LIVES

From Loui Giglio & Passion City Church

# John 4:1-26

Now Jesus learned that the Pharisees had heard that he was gaining and baptizing more disciples than John— 2 although in fact it was not Jesus who baptized, but his disciples. 3 So he left Judea and went back once more to Galilee.

4 Now he had to go through Samaria. 5 So he came to a town in Samaria called Sychar, near the plot of ground Jacob had given to his son Joseph. 6 Jacob's well was there, and Jesus, tired as he was from the journey, sat down by the well. It was about noon.

7 When a Samaritan woman came to draw water, Jesus said to her, "Will you give me a drink?" 8 (His disciples had gone into the town to buy food.)

9 The Samaritan woman said to him, "You are a Jew and I am a Samaritan woman. How can you ask me for a drink?" (For Jews do not associate with Samaritans.)
10 Jesus answered her, "If you knew the gift of God and who it is that asks you for a drink, you would have asked him and he would have given you living water."

11 "Sir," the woman said, "you have nothing to draw with and the well is deep. Where can you get this living water? 12 Are you greater than our father Jacob, who gave us the well and drank from it himself, as did also his sons and his livestock?"

13 Jesus answered, "Everyone who drinks this water will be thirsty again, 14 but whoever drinks the water I give them will never thirst. Indeed, the water I give them will become in them a spring of water welling up to eternal life."

15 The woman said to him, "Sir, give me this water so that I won't get thirsty and have to keep coming here to draw water."
16 He told her, "Go, call your husband and come back."

17 "I have no husband," she replied.

Jesus said to her, "You are right when you say you have no husband. 18 The fact is, you have had five husbands, and the man you now have is not your husband. What you have just said is quite true."

19 "Sir," the woman said, "I can see that you are a prophet. 20 Our ancestors worshiped on this mountain, but you Jews claim that the place where we must worship is in Jerusalem."
21 "Woman," Jesus replied, "believe me, a time is coming when you will worship the Father neither on this mountain nor in Jerusalem. 22 You Samaritans worship what you do not know; we worship what we do know, for salvation is from the Jews. 23 Yet a time is coming and has now come when the true worshipers will worship the Father in the Spirit and in truth, for they are the kind of worshipers the Father seeks. 24 God is spirit, and his worshipers must worship in the Spirit and in truth."

25 The woman said, "I know that Messiah" (called Christ) "is coming. When he comes, he will explain everything to us."

26 Then Jesus declared, "I, the one speaking to you—I am he."

# GROUP DISCUSSION:

After reading through John 4:1-26, discuss the following questions in your group

Why do you think the woman was coming to the well alone in the heat of the day?

Do we sometimes isolate ourselves because of sin?

Jesus met the woman right where she was—in her mess, her questions, her brokenness. Can you think of a time when Jesus met you in an unexpected or deeply personal way? What did that do in your heart?

The woman went from avoiding people to running into town to tell everyone about Jesus. How does encountering Jesus free us from shame and give us boldness to share our testimony?

Why do you think personal stories (like the woman's testimony) are so powerful in helping others come to know Jesus? What's one part of your story that you think God might use to impact someone else?

If someone asked you today, "Who is Jesus to you?"—what would you say, and how would your life back it up?

# Your Testimony

Use the guide below to help write out your story of a life-changing encounter with the risen Savior. ( Use the next few pages if you need more room)

| Before |  |
|---|---|
| Think about the void you had in your life and what you tried to fill it with before Jesus | |

| How |  |
|---|---|
| What caused you to turn to Jesus? | |

| After |  |
|---|---|
| How is your life different now with Jesus? | |

**MEMORY VERSE** ISAIAH 26:3 " YOU WILL KEEP IN PERFECT PEACE THOES WHOS MINDS ARE STEAD FAST, BECAUSE THEY TRUST IN YOU

MONDAY

TUESDAY

WEDNESDAY

**ACCOUNTABILITY PARTNER**_____

THURSDAY

FRIDAY

SATURDAY

SUNDAY

# DAILY DEVOTIONS

## WEEK 1

---

# TESTIMONY

I WAS ONE WAY, NOW I AM
COMPLETELY DIFFERENT,
AND THE THING THAT
HAPPENED IN BETWEEN IS
JESUS
-THE CHOSEN

# HE KNOWS ME

*Scripture: John 1:43-50*

*John 1:48*
*"How do you know me?" Nathanael*
*asked.*
*Jesus answered, "I saw you while you*
*were still under the fig tree before*
*Philip called you."*

Social media has made the world smaller. In some cases, that can be a good thing, like when I got to send a copy of my first book to Matt, whose book helped my family through a hard season of our lives. While that connection would not have been impossible without social media, it would have been very unlikely. When you use social media, you are inviting others into your life.

This passage in John teaches us that Jesus knew Nathanael before he ever met him. If this happened in 2025, Nathanael might have thought that Jesus stalked him on social media. Thankfully, this was not an option in the first century. Because of that, we see an essential truth about God: he saw us and moved towards us before we ever noticed him. That truth is an Integral part of our testimony. We did not have to message or post about our struggle to let him know we exist. He knew already!

This truth can be very humbling. God does not just know us outwardly; he knows who we truly are. That means he knows all the good and all the bad. The beauty in that is that he knows all of it and still calls us to himself. More than calling us, he died so that we can have a way back into right standing with God.

## Reflection Questions and Prayer

How was it meeting someone you really looked up to?
Would you be blown away knowing they knew about you?
When you realize the God of the universe sees you, how does that make you feel?
Read Isaiah 40 through the lens that God sees you, and knows what you are facing.

### A.C.T.S. Prayer

# SCRIPTURE STUDY

## John 1:43-50

Read through the passage above and use the questions
below to help you dive deeper into God's word

| | |
|---|---|
| (1) | **What did you observe in the passage?**<br>**What did I see?**<br>**What was the author saying?** |

| | |
|---|---|
| (2) | **What does the author mean by what he is saying?**<br>**What truth rises out of the text?** |

| | |
|---|---|
| (3) | **How Do I apply the truth from God's word?** |

# I WAS THERE

*Scripture: John 2:1-12*

### John 2:11
What Jesus did here in Cana of Galilee was the
first of the signs through which he revealed his
glory; and his disciples believed in him.

Sports have always been a big part of my life. I have great memories of when I was at a game and my team won. On the flip side, I have horrible memories of games where my team lost. Worse, I have memories from when they lost on the last play. The process is a roller coaster of emotions I would not wish on anyone.

November 30th, 2013, was a dark day for my beloved Alabama Crimson Tide. It was the day that the Auburn Tigers, our in-state rivals, beat us by returning a missed field goal for 109 yards. It still hurts to this day to even think about it. I can't be certain, but I think some of the gray in my hair came from that night.

The Worst part about that game is that every college football broadcast seems to love to show clips of that play. It is a cruel and unusual form of punishment. In my opinion, I never played as nap of that game. I was not a staff or even a student at the university, but I can still tell you all about that moment. It is permanently burned in my memory.

Jesus' disciples had a similar experience with the wedding in John chapter 2. It was not their wedding, nor did they do anything to partake in the miracle. They did, however, have a testimony to tell about Jesus' goodness and greatness. Testimonies are what we have seen God do in our lives and around us. Just like the disciples, we can testify about what we have seen God do in our lives and those around us.

## Reflection Questions & Prayer

When have you seen God show up and show out in the lives of someone around you?
Do you think the goodness of God is only your story to tell when it involves you?
Is the point of any testimony to point people to you or God?
Who have you told lately about the goodness of God?

## A.C.T.S. Prayer

# SCRIPTURE STUDY

# John 2:1-12

Read through the passage above and use the questions below to help you dive deeper into God's word

**1**
**What did you observe in the passage?**
**What did I see?**
**What was the author saying?**

**2**
**What does the author mean by what he is saying?**
**What truth rises out of the text?**

**3**
**How Do I apply the truth from God's word?**

# GROUP PROJECT

*Scripture: John 3:1-21*

*John 3:3*

*Jesus replied, "Very truly I tell you, no one can see the kingdom of God unless they are born again."*

Have you ever had a group project in class or at work, and you know that one of the group members will do absolutely nothing? They put in no effort and get full credit. This scenario is part of our testimony, and the bad thing is that we are the ones who do none of the work. We get to receive the full credit for the work Jesus did.

In John chapter 3, we see a conversation between Jesus and Nicodemus. Jesus tells Nicodemus that no one can see the kingdom of God unless they are born again (John3:3). The crazy thing about birth is that you are a part of the story, but you do none of the work. You celebrate the day every year, and you did 0% of the work from creation to grand entry into the world.

Yet every year, people give you presents, and they let you make a wish and blow the candles out on the cake. I can't speak for you, but I don't ever remember a time when I did not accept and receive the presents and cake with open arms. The same is true for our testimony to God. Yes, it involves us, and we are the recipients of the work done. That is the narrative of our salvation story. Jesus did the job and offers us the credit he earned. The only thing required of us is to accept his gift.

## Reflection Questions & Prayer

When you tell the story of your testimony, who is the main character?
What do you feel led to do when you hear that you did nothing to earn your salvation?
Does understanding this truth impact the way you worship Jesus?

**A.C.T.S. Prayer**

# SCRIPTURE STUDY

## John 3:1-21

Read through the passage above and use the questions
below to help you dive deeper into God's word

| 1 | What did you observe in the passage?<br>What did I see?<br>What was the author saying? |
|---|---|
|   |   |

| 2 | What does the author mean by what he is saying?<br>What truth rises out of the text? |
|---|---|
|   |   |

| 3 | How Do I apply the truth from God's word? |
|---|---|
|   |   |

# DO YOU WANT TO BE HEALED?

*Scripture: John 5:1-15*

*John 5:6*
*When Jesus saw him lying there and learned that he had been in this condition for a long time, he asked him, "Do you want to get well?"*

It is no secret that the world we live in is very broken. If you don't believe me, just turn on a major news outlet. The content you will see will typically not make you feel warm and fuzzy in your soul. If you are not a news watcher, just scroll through social media. It does not matter if it is national news or local town drama; the content is slanted toward the negative.

Part of the burden we live with in this world is disease. Over the past decade, I have seen people I know lose loved ones to childhood cancer, ALS, genetic disorders, heart disease, and mental illness. Sadly, many of the diseases we live with do not have cures. Some diseases we live with have terminal diagnoses, while some just cause life to be more difficult.

I have watched my mom live with rheumatoid arthritis for the majority of my life. While I am thankful the disease is not terminal, I do know it has made parts of life a struggle for her. I can't speak for her, but I know if someone asked me if I wanted a cure for my mom to make her life better, I would say yes in a heartbeat.

Part of our testimony is realizing we are all suffering from the disease of sin. The diagnosis, unfortunately, is terminal. Luckily, God sees our disease and offers us a cure. The only question for us is whether we will accept it. While this may sound silly, people pass by this cure every day and choose to live with the disease. One of the biggest threads in our testimony's story is that we knew the diagnosis, and our God gave us a cure!

## Reflection Questions & Prayer

If you had cancer and someone gave you a cure, would you take it?
Would you tell people about the cure and the person who gave it to you?
Who have you told about Jesus, the one who saves you from your sin, lately?

A.C.T.S. Prayer

# SCRIPTURE STUDY

# John 5:1-15

Read through the passage above and use the questions
below to help you dive deeper into God's word

| 1 | **What did you observe in the passage?**<br>**What did I see?**<br>**What was the author saying?** |
|---|---|

| 2 | **What does the author mean by what he is saying?**<br>**What truth rises out of the text?** |
|---|---|

| 3 | **How Do I apply the truth from God's word?** |
|---|---|

# BORN THIS WAY

*Scripture: John 9:1-15*

*John 9:11*
*He replied, "The man they call Jesus made*
*some mud and put it on my eyes. He told me*
*to go to Siloam and wash. So I went and*
*washed, and then I could see."*

While hard work, training, and dedication can help you excel, some things are out of our control. We can work and wish all we want, but it does not change the reality of our situation. Some things we are just born with. Whether it is physical traits or medical issues, some of the things we deal with are not our fault, but they are our problem.

What if a simple interaction with someone could change the way we were born? What if it did not just change the way you were born, but transformed you into something completely different? This is the story of any follower of Jesus. Not only are we different because of Jesus, but we are different in the best possible way.

It was not the mud or the water that restored the man's sight in John 9. It was his interaction with the Son of God. You can't skip over the fact that his sight was restored when he trusted Jesus and did what he said. The man in the story had a choice: to do what Jesus said or to walk away. That same choice is the one that every person on earth is faced with.

This is a part of every believer's testimony. It was not the sermon or the music playing in church. It was not the coffee shop where someone shared Jesus with you. You came to salvation by trusting and following Jesus as Lord and Savior. The man in the story did not testify about the mud or the water, but he testified about the one who told him what to do.

## Reflection Questions & Prayer

How does hope in Jesus change how you approach and view life?
Is that hope your light in the darkness, or are you looking to other things? Have you shared that hope with someone who is walking in the darkness?

## A.C.T.S. Prayer

# SCRIPTURE STUDY

# John 9:1-15

Read through the passage above and use the questions
below to help you dive deeper into God's word

---

**1**     **What did you observe in the passage?**
**What did I see?**
**What was the author saying?**

---

**2**     **What does the author mean by what he is saying?**
**What truth rises out of the text?**

---

**3**     **How Do I apply the truth from God's word?**

# I RAN OUT OF THAT GRAVE

*Scripture: John 11:1-44*

*John 11:43-44*
43 When he had said this, Jesus called in a loud voice, "Lazarus, come out!" 44 The dead man came out, his hands and feet wrapped with strips of linen, and a cloth around his face.
Jesus said to them, "Take off the grave clothes and let him go."

I remember when I was little, it did not matter what I was doing, or where I was at, when I heard my parents yell my name, I moved towards it. If you did not come when they called, then you were going to be in trouble. The choice was simple: run to see what they wanted or ignore it and face the consequences. Usually, you could tell by the tone and how many names they used if they were calling you to something good, or if you were in trouble.

Responding to Jesus' call is another central theme of any believer's testimony. Just like Lazarus, we were all in the grave because of our sin. When God called our names, we all had a choice. We could either move toward him out of the grave, or we could ignore it and stay where we are.

One of the beautiful things that I see in John 11 is that Jesus does not leave Lazarus in his grave clothes. The same is true for us. We don't have to walk around in things from our old life. All of those things belong in the grave. Part of our testimony is sharing how we moved on from things of our old life to the new life in Jesus.

## Reflection Questions & Prayer

What parts of your old life have you left in the grave? (Take a second to praise God that those things are not who you are anymore)
What parts of your old life do you need to leave in the grave?
Think about how amazing Jesus called you from death to life. Is this truth impacting how you live your life?

**A.C.T.S. Prayer**

# SCRIPTURE STUDY

# John 11:1-44

Read through the passage above and use the questions
below to help you dive deeper into God's word

---

**1**

**What did you observe in the passage?**
**What did I see?**
**What was the author saying?**

---

**2**

**What does the author mean by what he is saying?**
**What truth rises out of the text?**

---

**3**

**How Do I apply the truth from God's word?**

# JESUS AND OUR QUESTIONS

*Scripture: John 18:28-40*

### John 18:38
*"What is truth?" retorted Pilate. With this he went out
again to the Jews gathered there and said, "I find no basis
for a charge against him.*

Never ask a question that you are not prepared to hear the answer to. This is a great truth for anyone to live by, but especially for people who work with teenagers. They will gladly give you the cold, hard truth. Sometimes, they will even give youth at truth when you don't even ask a question.

Today's scripture shows the Roman leader over Judea, Pilate, questioning Jesus after his arrest. After questioning Jesus, Pilate finds no fault in him and does not believe he is deserving of death. The interesting part of this exchange is how Jesus answers his questions.

Jesus never pleaded with Pilate to save him. He also never seemed rattled or nervous about the examination. It is easy to see the confidence in Jesus' response. That confidence comes from knowing who he is and what he came to do.

Part of our testimony is coming to the realization that Pilate did. This man named Jesus was innocent and willingly took on the cross to make a way for us. So don't be shy about bringing your questions to God. He knows who he is, what he has done, and what he will do. Also, don't be scared of others' questions about God. He has an excellent track record when dealing with the questions of unbelievers.

## Reflection Questions & Prayer

What questions have you been scared to ask God?
How has holding onto those questions been affecting/ impacting your life and
relationship with Jesus?
Do you believe that Jesus is "the truth" and that what he says is 100% true?

### A.C.T.S. Prayer

# SCRIPTURE STUDY

## John 18:28-40

Read through the passage above and use the questions below
to help you dive deeper into God's word

| 1 | **What did you observe in the passage?**<br>**What did I see?**<br>**What was the author saying?** |
|---|---|
| | |

| 2 | **What does the author mean by what he is saying?**<br>**What truth rises out of the text?** |
|---|---|
| | |

| 3 | **How Do I apply the truth from God's word?** |
|---|---|
| | |

# CAPTIVATED

Week 2

C.S LEWIS

# WHEN CHRIST DIED, HE DIED FOR YOU INDIVIDUALLY JUST AS MUCH AS IF YOU'D BEEN THE ONLY MAN IN THE WORLD.

Isaiah 53:2 *" He grew up before him like a tender shoot, and like a root out of dry ground. He had no beauty or majesty to attract us to him, nothing in his appearance that we should desire him."*

What is the most beautiful thing you have ever seen? Something that was just so overwhelming that you could not take your eyes off of it. For me, the moment I think of is the moment I saw Gena walking down the aisle on our wedding day. I hope that for the rest of my time on this side of heaven, I will always be able to remember that day.

Calling the 24 hours leading up to that moment chaotic is an understatement. I just wanted to give you the rundown. We were getting married in a barn in Snead, Alabama. Cotton fields surrounded it, and they promised to leave the cotton until after the wedding. It was picked the day before the wedding. On top of that, it was bone-chilling cold with winds of 30-40 miles per hour. The worst part was that one of our best friends and a member of the wedding party lost his dad the night of our rehearsal.

However, no matter all the things that surrounded our wedding, nothing could pull my attention from Gena as she walked down the aisle. I was captivated by her that day. All these years later, I am more captivated by her than I was on our wedding day. This is the same reason that will help us become more captivated with Jesus. The more I know Gena, the more I realize how awesome she is. I say this with all the love in my heart, she does not compare to Jesus.

As we see who Jesus is and grow closer to him, the old hymn "Turn your eyes upon Jesus" will ring true in our lives. It says, "And things of this world will grow strangely dim, in the light of his goodness and grace". That is our goal for this section of the study. To become more captivated with Jesus by studying who he is. This week's devotion will cover the 7 "I am" statements Jesus makes—what better way to get to know him than by exploring how he describes himself. While the world will say Jesus was nothing special, his followers know that special only begins to describe him.

# Matthew 16:13-28

13 When Jesus came to the region of Caesarea Philippi, he asked his disciples, "Who do people say the Son of Man is?"

14 They replied, "Some say John the Baptist; others say Elijah; and still others, Jeremiah or one of the prophets."

15 "But what about you?" he asked. "Who do you say I am?"
16 Simon Peter answered, "You are the Messiah, the Son of the living God."

17 Jesus replied, "Blessed are you, Simon son of Jonah, for this was not revealed to you by flesh and blood, but by my Father in heaven. 18 And I tell you that you are Peter,[b] and on this rock I will build my church, and the gates of Hades[c] will not overcome it. 19 I will give you the keys of the kingdom of heaven; whatever you bind on earth will be[d] bound in heaven, and whatever you loose on earth will be[e] loosed in heaven." 20 Then he ordered his disciples not to tell anyone that he was the Messiah. 21 From that time on Jesus began to explain to his disciples that he must go to Jerusalem and suffer many things at the hands of the elders, the chief priests and the teachers of the law, and that he must be killed and on the third day be raised to life.

22 Peter took him aside and began to rebuke him. "Never, Lord!" he said. "This shall never happen to you!"

23 Jesus turned and said to Peter, "Get behind me, Satan! You are a stumbling block to me; you do not have in mind the concerns of God, but merely human concerns."

24 Then Jesus said to his disciples, "Whoever wants to be my disciple must deny themselves and take up their cross and follow me. 25 For whoever wants to save their life[f] will lose it, but whoever loses their life for me will find it. 26 What good will it be for someone to gain the whole world, yet forfeit their soul? Or what can anyone give in exchange for their soul? 27 For the Son of Man is going to come in his Father's glory with his angels, and then he will reward each person according to what they have done.

28 "Truly I tell you, some who are standing here will not taste death before they see the Son of Man coming in his kingdom."

# GROUP DISCUSSION:

After reading through Matthew 16:13-28 discuss the following questions in your group

**What are the ways people around the world would describe Jesus?**

**What difference does it make in your life by claiming Jesus as the messiah instead of a prophet?**

**What does Peter's response—"You are the Christ, the Son of the living God"—reveal about his understanding of Jesus? How would you personally answer that question today?**

**Jesus goes from praising Peter's faith to rebuking him—why do you think Jesus reacted so strongly when Peter tried to stop Him from talking about His suffering and death? What does that teach us about following Jesus on His terms, not ours?**

**What are some things in our lives that distract us or compete with our awe and focus on Jesus? How can we re-center our hearts on Him?**

**MEMORY VERSE** MATTHEW 16:16 "SIMON PETER ANSWERED, "YOU ARE THE MESSIAH, THE SON OF THE LIVING GOD."

MONDAY

TUESDAY

WEDNESDAY

**ACCOUNTABILITY PARTNER**_____

**THURSDAY**

**FRIDAY**

**SATURDAY**

**SUNDAY**

# DAILY DEVOTIONS

## WEEK 2

# CAPTIVATED

"BEHOLD THE LAMB OF GOD
WHO TAKES AWAY THE SIN
OF THE WORLD."
JOHN THE BAPTIST

# BREAD OF LIFE

*Scripture: John 6:25-59*

**John 6:26**
*"Jesus answered, "Very truly I tell you, you are looking for
me, not because you saw the signs I performed but
because you ate the loaves and had your fill.*

Point Break was a movie in the early 90's about adrenaline junkies who are also criminals and an undercover FBI agent. The main antagonist, Bodhi, has a famous line in the movie where he says, "Life at the edge is the only life worth living. You haven't felt alive until you have taken it to the limit". While this is a fictional movie, many people apply this thinking.

The desire to be full, or to have life to the fullest, is something that everyone goes after. However, people go about achieving it in different ways. Some believe that they will be satisfied if they have enough money in their bank account or 401(k). Others think they will find fulfillment if they have the right job title or position. Then you have people who look to take life to the limits through substances and the reaction they get from them. No matter the case, all of these things will leave you empty and longing for absolute satisfaction.

Jesus said in John chapter 6 that he is the bread that comes down from heaven. Not only will he satisfy you on this side of heaven, but you will have eternal life. The catalyst to Jesus being the bread of life comes in verse 47 where Jesus says, "Very truly I tell you, the one who believes has eternal life.". The belief that through Jesus' life, death, and resurrection, we are made right with God is the only place to find fulfillment for our biggest desire.

## Reflection Questions & Prayer

What do you look to, hoping to find fulfillment other than Jesus Though Jesus' teaching might be hard, are you walking in or away from it?
Do you believe that Jesus is who Peter said he was in verses 68-69 If you answer No, what is keeping you from that?

## A.C.T.S. Prayer

# SCRIPTURE STUDY

## John 6:25-59

Read through the passage above and use the questions
below to help you dive deeper into God's word

---

**1**

**What did you observe in the passage?**
**What did I see?**
**What was the author saying?**

---

**2**

**What does the author mean by what he is saying?**
**What truth rises out of the text?**

---

**3**

**How Do I apply the truth from God's word?**

# LIGHT OF THE WORLD

*Scripture: John 8:1-20*

*John 8:12*
*"When Jesus spoke again to the people, he said, "I am
the light of the world. Whoever follows me will never
walk in darkness, but will have the light of life."*

Light is an interesting and essential part of our lives that we often never even consider. For instance, light is so fast that it could circle the Earth more than seven times in one second. The colors we see are sult of the different wave lengths of light. While light allows us to see, we can't even know every part of light. Infrared, ultraviolet, and microwaves are all beyond the visible light we can see.

Darkness, on the other hand, is not its own thing. Darkness is the absence of light. We are not made for complete darkness. In complete darkness, we can become disoriented and start to hallucinate. This is because our brains rely heavily on visual input.
While we may not understand everything about light and its workings, we need it. Take a child and let them walk in to a dark house. They will know they need to find the light to turn on so they can see. They know they don't belong in the dark. Nor do they want to be there any longer than they have to.

The same is true for us spiritually. Because of our sin, we are born into darkness. Luckily, that is not where we belong, and God does not want to leave us there. Jesus said, "I am the light of the world". The beauty of his statement is what the light came to show us. At the end of verse 12 in chapter 8, Jesus says, "whoever follows me will never walk in darkness, but will have the light of life". As long as we walk in darkness, we will never find the life we were made to have. To make it to the desired destination, we must follow the light.

## Reflection Questions & Prayer

We can see more clearly as we get closer to a light source. What does moving closer to Jesus help us see in our lives?
What parts of your life are you scared to let Jesus into, because you know what you will see when you do?
How does obeying Jesus' command to follow him keep us from falling into the darkness of this world?

**A.C.T.S. Prayer**

# SCRIPTURE STUDY

# John 8:1-20

Read through the passage above and use the questions
below to help you dive deeper into God's word

| 1 | **What did you observe in the passage?** <br> **What did I see?** <br> **What was the author saying?** |
|---|---|

| 2 | **What does the author mean by what he is saying?** <br> **What truth rises out of the text?** |
|---|---|

| 3 | **How Do I apply the truth from God's word?** |
|---|---|

# THE GATE

*John 10:10*
*"The thief comes only to steal and kill and destroy; I have come that they may have life, and have it to the full."*

When fall hit the South, one of the traditions I remember from my time as a teenager was going to corn mazes that were "haunted." The concept was pretty straightforward: Send a group of people out into a maze cut into a cornfield at night, all while people were placed in the maze trying to scare you.

While I don't remember being scared too much, I do remember getting really lost. Like so, lost we were hoping to find someone trying to scare us so we could ask them how to get back to the start. It started out as fun trying to find our way, but it quickly disappeared when we had no clue where we were or how to return to our parents waiting in the car.

Some people treat finding God like going through a corn maze, hoping that if they take the right path, they will end up at the desired destination. Just like all roads don't lead to the end of the maze, all paths of life don't lead to heaven. It's eternally significant that we find the right way.

It is in Jesus and Jesus alone that we find life. Our works don't make a door to God for us. Jesus is the gate to eternal life and freely offers us entry. While the thief comes to kill, steal, and destroy, Jesus is not trying to take from us but to give us life to the fullest

## Reflection Questions & Prayer

What are some things in this world you are looking to other than Jesus to give you life?
Do you find fulfillment in those things, or do they leave you wanting more?
What did it cost Jesus to make the gate for us? Why is it important for us to remember that?

## A.C.T.S. Prayer

# SCRIPTURE STUDY

# John 10:1-10

Read through the passage above and use the questions
below to help you dive deeper into God's word

| 1 | **What did you observe in the passage?**<br>**What did I see?**<br>**What was the author saying?** |
|---|---|
| | |

| 2 | **What does the author mean by what he is saying?**<br>**What truth rises out of the text?** |
|---|---|
| | |

| 3 | **How Do I apply the truth from God's word?** |
|---|---|
| | |

# THE GOOD SHEPARD

*Scripture: John 10:11-21*

*John 10:11*
*"I am the good shepherd. The good shepherd lays
down his life for the sheep. "*

One of the best memories I have during my teaching career is walking my kids to school. I have had many moments where I have had to just pause and thank God for his goodness and the things he has blessed me with. I have also had moments where I have learned things about my heavenly father while being a father to my girls.

One of those moments happened after Emory Kate asked me a question one day. Every day, when we walk from the parking lot onto the sidewalk, I always move her to the other side of me from the cars dropping students off. One day, she asked me why I did that. I told her I wanted to ensure I was between her and the danger to keep her safe.

It is the shepherd's job to take care of the sheep—not only to lead them to good places where they can thrive, but also to protect them from the dangers of the world. This is exactly what Jesus does for us. He leads us beside still waters and stands between us and the dangers of life. That's why following Jesus is not a jail cell for us to live in, but guardrails to protect us from danger.

## Reflection Questions & Prayer

Why is Jesus our "good" shepherd instead of just a shepherd? Can you trust someone who would lay down their life for you?
What areas of your life are you not trusting your good shepherd?

### A.C.T.S. Prayer

# SCRIPTURE STUDY

# John 10:11-21

Read through the passage above and use the questions
below to help you dive deeper into God's word

| 1 | **What did you observe in the passage?**<br>**What did I see?**<br>**What was the author saying?** |
|---|---|
| | |

| 2 | **What does the author mean by what he is saying?**<br>**What truth rises out of the text?** |
|---|---|
| | |

| 3 | **How Do I apply the truth from God's word?** |
|---|---|
| | |

# THE RESURECTION AND LIFE

*Scripture: John 11-1-44*

*John 11:25*
*"Jesus said to her, "I am the resurrection and the life. The one who believes in me will live, even though they die;"*

My wife is a real-life superhero. For the first part of her career as a nurse, she worked in the emergency room, tending to the sick and injured and assisting in bringing people back from the brink of death. Her stories of saving someone who had no heartbeat and was not breathing somehow always trumped my stories of giving kids ISS (in-school suspension) or a break detention form in or offences.

While being a real-life hero, my wife did not invent the life-saving measures they used in the emergency room. Mouth-to-mouth resuscitation was first suggested for drowning victims by the Paris Academy of Science in 1740. Many techniques used for CPR today have been added throughout the centuries. However, no matter how skilled you are at CPR, that does you no good in a graveyard.

While we can help bring someone back from the brink of death, Jesus is the only one who can bring someone back from actual death. This is an integral part of who Jesus is for his followers. You are not just putting your faith in someone who is a good teacher. You are putting your faith in and following the one who is over death and the grave! He tells us that and proves it by paying our price on the cross and leaving the grave three days later.

## Reflection Questions & Prayer

Knowing Jesus can call the dead back to life, how can that information impact your prayer life?
What areas of your life are you needing Jesus to call you out of the grave and into new life?
How does knowing Jesus felt emotions like us impact how you look at him?
**A.C.T.S. Prayer**

# SCRIPTURE STUDY

# John 11:1-44

Read through the passage above and use the questions below to
help you dive deeper into God's word

| | |
|---|---|
| 1 | **What did you observe in the passage?**<br>**What did I see?**<br>**What was the author saying?** |

| | |
|---|---|
| 2 | **What does the author mean by what he is saying?**<br>**What truth rises out of the text?** |

| | |
|---|---|
| 3 | **How Do I apply the truth from God's word?** |

# THE WAY, TRUTH, AND LIFE

*Scripture: John 14:1-14*

*John 14:6*
*" Jesus answered, "I am the way and the truth and the life. No one comes to the Father except through me."*

One of the best illustrations I have heard for sharing that Jesus is the way came from pastor Jonathan Pokluda. He says, "Imagine you are at the world's largest air port in Saudi Arabia, and you have a sick child. You need to get them home, but you have no idea which plane will take you there. So you ask someone and they say," Pick any of them and they will get you where you need to go". We know that's not how it works. Not all planes carry you where you need to go, just like not all roads lead to heaven.

In John14, we see Jesus comforting his disciples. He tells them they know the way to the place he is going. Thomas (like many of us would) told Jesus, "Hey, man, we don't know where you are going. "Then, Jesus makes one of the biggest "I am" statements to his disciples. Jesus is our way!

He is our way back to the Father's house. He is the truth we can walk in, knowing he is not deceiving us. He tells us exactly what we get with him.....life. While we don't know what will happen next, we know that whether it is a hill or a valley, Jesus will be with us! We don't have to worry about where to go because we know The Way!

## Reflection Questions & Prayer

How does knowing Jesus is the way to God offer comfort for us?
How does knowing that not all roads lead to heaven help you answer Jesus' call to go and make disciples?
How does following Jesus keep us from the enemy's deception (satan)?

## A.C.T.S. Prayer

# SCRIPTURE STUDY

## John 14:1-14

Read through the passage above and use the questions
below to help you dive deeper into God's word

| 1 | **What did you observe in the passage?**<br>**What did I see?**<br>**What was the author saying?** |
|---|---|
| | |

| 2 | **What does the author mean by what he is saying?**<br>**What truth rises out of the text?** |
|---|---|
| | |

| 3 | **How Do I apply the truth from God's word?** |
|---|---|
| | |

# THE VINE

*Scripture: John 15:1-17*

**John 15:5**
*I am the vine; you are the branches. If you remain in
me and I in you, you will bear much fruit; apart from
me, you can do nothing.*

In science, we learn about producers and consumers. Producers can make their food, while consumers have to eat producers or other consumers for food. Even though producers can make their food through photosynthesis, they still rely on the sun. Without the sun, the process does not happen. That is true for us spiritually; we depend upon the Son, not the sun.

We see in John 15 that Jesus makes a straightforward statement in verse 4. Jesus says, "No branch can bear fruit by itself; it must remain in the vine." You don't need to be a biology major to know that if you cut the branch off the apple tree, the branch stops producing apples. It must stay connected to the tree to keep producing apples.

The point Jesus is making is one that we all need to pay attention to. If we want to see the fruit of God in our lives, we must stay connected to him and do what he tells us to do. This leads us to an important question we must ask ourselves periodically. Can I see the fruit of God in my life? If the answer is no, then we must check to see if we have been connected to him. We are not abiding in him if we do not keep his commands.

## Reflection Questions & Prayer

Abide simply means to stay or dwell. Looking at your life over the last few months, have you been abiding in Jesus?
All fruit starts big; it has to grow. What small ways are you growing in Jesus that you can see in your life?
What do you need to ask God to remove that keeps you from being fruitful?

## A.C.T.S. Prayer

# SCRIPTURE STUDY
# John 15:1-17

Read through the passage above and use the questions
below to help you dive deeper into God's word

| 1 | **What did you observe in the passage?** <br> **What did I see?** <br> **What was the author saying?** |
|---|---|

| 2 | **What does the author mean by what he is saying?** <br> **What truth rises out of the text?** |
|---|---|

| 3 | **How Do I apply the truth from God's word?** |
|---|---|

# CULTIVATED

Week 3

LOUIE GIGLIO

# JESUS MUST INCREASE AND I MUST DECREASE

2nd Timothy 3:16-17 "<u>All Scripture is God-breathed and is useful for teaching, rebuking, correcting and training in righteousness, 17 so that the servant of God[a] may be thoroughly equipped for every good work.</u>"

If you Google the definition for cultivate, two options will come up. The first is to prepare or use the land for crops or gardening. The second definition is to acquire or develop a skill or quality. While you may have never cultivated land before, you have gone through the cultivation process before.

We go through cultivation at school when we acquire skills and knowledge. We cultivate our bodies through diet and exercise. We also cultivate our skill set by learning and developing our talent in athletics and the arts. However, cultivation is not just limited to our physical selves. We grow our bank account through investments. These are just a few examples of how we use the process of cultivation in our lives.

Sanctification is a word we hear in church but typically don't understand. It is simply the process of becoming more like Jesus by moving further away from our sins. This does not happen through a one-time event but rather through a process of growing in Jesus. The teaching of Jesus is one of the biggest tools to help us learn how to follow Him.

Jesus was an excellent teacher during his time on earth. One of the ways he taught the people was through parables. A parable is a simple story using ordinary things to help teach a spiritual lesson. For this section, we are going to look at the parables of Jesus to see the lessons we can apply to our lives to help us look more like him.

# Mark 4:1-20

Again Jesus began to teach by the lake. The crowd that gathered around him was so large that he got into a boat and sat in it out on the lake, while all the people were along the shore at the water's edge. 2 He taught them many things by parables, and in his teaching said: 3 "Listen! A farmer went out to sow his seed. 4 As he was scattering the seed, some fell along the path, and the birds came and ate it up. 5 Some fell on rocky places, where it did not have much soil. It sprang up quickly, because the soil was shallow. 6 But when the sun came up, the plants were scorched, and they withered because they had no root. 7 Other seed fell among thorns, which grew up and choked the plants, so that they did not bear grain. 8 Still other seed fell on good soil. It came up, grew and produced a crop, some multiplying thirty, some sixty, some a hundred times."

9 Then Jesus said, "Whoever has ears to hear, let them hear."
10 When he was alone, the Twelve and the others around him asked him about the parables. 11 He told them, "The secret of the kingdom of God has been given to you. But to those on the outside everything is said in parables 12 so that,
"'they may be ever seeing but never perceiving,
    and ever hearing but never understanding;
otherwise they might turn and be forgiven!'[a]"

13 Then Jesus said to them, "Don't you understand this parable? How then will you understand any parable? 14 The farmer sows the word. 15 Some people are like seed along the path, where the word is sown. As soon as they hear it, Satan comes and takes away the word that was sown in them. 16 Others, like seed sown on rocky places, hear the word and at once receive it with joy. 17 But since they have no root, they last only a short time. When trouble or persecution comes because of the word, they quickly fall away. 18 Still others, like seed sown among thorns, hear the word; 19 but the worries of this life, the deceitfulness of wealth and the desires for other things come in and choke the word, making it unfruitful.

20 Others, like seed sown on good soil, hear the word, accept it, and produce a crop—some thirty, some sixty, some a hundred times what was sown."

# GROUP DISCUSSION:

After reading through Mark 4:1-20 discuss the following questions in your group

In the Parable of the Sower, Jesus describes different heart conditions. What kind of soil best describes your heart when you first encountered Jesus?

How has that changed over time? What caused that change?

Jesus says the Kingdom of God is like a tiny seed that grows into something powerful and life-giving. Can you share about a "small beginning" in your walk with Jesus that grew into something meaningful?

Verses 16–17 describe people who receive the word with joy but fall away when trouble comes. Have you ever had a season like that? What helped bring you back to a deeper faith?

The good soil produces a crop that multiplies. Can you think of a moment in your life when God's Word really took root and began to change you—or even impact others through you?

**MEMORY VERSE**  2ND TIMOTHY 3:16-17 "ALL SCRIPTURE IS GOD-BREATHED AND IS USEFUL FOR TEACHING, REBUKING, CORRECTING AND TRAINING IN RIGHTEOUSNESS, 17 SO THAT THE SERVANT OF GOD MAY BE THOROUGHLY EQUIPPED FOR EVERY GOOD WORK.

MONDAY

TUESDAY

WEDNESDAY

**ACCOUNTABILITY PARTNER**_____

( )

**THURSDAY**

**FRIDAY**

**SATURDAY**

**SUNDAY**

# DAILY DEVOTIONS
## WEEK 3

---

# CULTIVATED

---

"PARABLES ARE LIKE SHELLS
THAT KEEP GOOD FRUIT FOR
THE DILIGENT, BUT KEEP IT
FROM THE LAZY."
MATTHEW HENERY

# WOODEN'S ADVICE

*Scripture: Luke 10:25-37*

**Luke 10:29**
*But he wanted to justify himself, so he asked Jesus,*
*"And who is my neighbor?"*

How far would you go to help out a family member who was in trouble? I would like to think I would like to think I would be like Liam Neeson in the movie Taken. If you have not seen that movie, he moves heaven and earth and disposes of anyone who stands in his way from getting to his daughter with swift violence. For someone we love, that is not a far stretch.

What about for someone who is your enemy? How you would respond could vary. If they need twenty dollars for gas, you might find it in your heart to do that. If they need a kidney, that might be out of the question. This way of thinking is just the nature of our humanity.

In the story of the good Samaritan, Jesus shows us what it really looks like to love your neighbor as yourself. The interesting thing about this parable of Jesus is that he made a Samaritan the story's hero while speaking to an audience full of Jewish people. In the story, the people who should have helped him did not because it would have cost them something.

John Wooden once said, "You can't live a perfect day without doing something for someone who will never be able to repay you". If we only help the ones who can help us, are we really helping at all? I believe that way is more of a quid pro quo system. I think the overarching theme of Jesus' parable is showing unconditional mercy and grace. God showed us mercy when we did not deserve it or could ever repay him. If we want to live like Jesus, that is precisely what we must do.

## Reflection Questions & Prayer

In the parable of the Good Samaritan, which man are you living your life like?
Have you ever felt God leading you to show compassion to someone? How did you respond?
What is keeping you from "going and doing likewise"?

**A.C.T.S. Prayer**

# SCRIPTURE STUDY

## Luke 10:25-37

Read through the passage above and use the questions
below to help you dive deeper into God's word

**1**

**What did you observe in the passage?**
**What did I see?**
**What was the author saying?**

**2**

**What does the author mean by what he is saying?**
**What truth rises out of the text?**

**3**

**How Do I apply the truth from God's word?**

# LOST AND FOUND

*Scripture: Luke 15*

*Luke 15:32*
*But we had to celebrate and be glad, because this brother of*
*yours was dead and is alive again; he was lost and is found.'"*

Have you ever lost something extremely important or valuable to you? May be it was a stuffed animal when you were a child. Or perhaps it was something of value you misplaced as an adult. How excited were you when you found that item? Was your reaction joyful or just business as usual?

On the flip side, have you ever lost something of not much value and found it? May be a set of keys to your car. Or the remote control for the television? While the world may not seem to recognize them as necessary, how did your actions in the search show they were important to you? Running through the house, looking above and under things. Flipping couch cushions and checking the pockets of clothes you have worn and the effort because you need and want that item.

In Luke 15, we see Jesus tell three parables about lost things being found and the reaction that causes the seeker of the items. These three parables respond to the religious leaders' asking why he eats with "sinners". While there religious leaders thought that the tax collectors and sinners were not worth eating with, Jesus shows the celebration in heaven when a lost sinner comes home.

Simply put, as followers of Jesus, we were all lost at one point. Jesus took on the cross and bore our sin and shame so we could find our life in him. Once we realize what it took for us to be found, it's easy to sing the words of the old hymn Amazing Grace: "I once was lost, but now I am found. I was blind, but now I see."

## Reflection Questions & Prayer

How does it make you feel knowing that God left the 99 to rescue you? Does this change how you see your self-worth or the value of your life?
As followers of Jesus, why is it important to reach out to and show love to people who are lost in their sin?

**A.C.T.S. Prayer**

# SCRIPTURE STUDY

# Luke 15

Read through the passage above and use the questions
below to help you dive deeper into God's word

**1**

**What did you observe in the passage?**
**What did I see?**
**What was the author saying?**

**2**

**What does the author mean by what he is saying?**
**What truth rises out of the text?**

**3**

**How Do I apply the truth from God's word?**

# BE A FOUNTAIN, NOT A DRAIN

*Scripture: Luke 12:13-21*

*Luke 12:15*
*Then he said to them, "Watch out! Be on your guard against all kinds of greed; life does not consist in an abundance of possessions.*

When you think of greed, what or who comes to mind? When I think about that greed, I think about Scrooge McDuck. He was a character on the cartoon Duck Tales. Scrounge was like Bill Gates rich, and he loved his money. This love caused him to want to hold onto and hoard all of his riches. Luckily for Scrooge, he realized there was more to life than money and possessions.

In our text for today, we see two brothers fighting over possessions. Jesus used this question to teach a lesson about the kingdom of God. In the story, we see someone blessed with a crop who needed to build bigger barns to hold all his possessions. This is not a bad problem to have, but he missed the source of his blessing.

Did you know that neither a fountain nor a drain is the source of water? They are only how the water is dispersed. Fountains take the water from the source and spread it out, while drains take the water in and send it away.

Psalm 24:1 says, "The world is the Lord's, and everything in it". So the most important thing to realize is that the source of our blessings comes from the Lord. After we realize that we must ask ourselves an important question: What am I doing with what the Lord blessed me with? Or simply are you being a fountain or a drain?

## Reflection Questions & Prayer

How can material things become idols that we worship?
Do you look at all the blessings in your life as a gift from God?
Have you asked God lately how you can use what he has given you for his kingdom and glory?

**A.C.T.S. Prayer**

# SCRIPTURE STUDY

# Luke 12:13-21

Read through the passage above and use the questions
below to help you dive deeper into God's word

**1** **What did you observe in the passage?**
**What did I see?**
**What was the author saying?**

**2** **What does the author mean by what he is saying?**
**What truth rises out of the text?**

**3** **How Do I apply the truth from God's word?**

# DON'T FORGET ABOUT THE BOOKS

*Scripture: Luke 6:46-49*

***Luke 6:46***
*"Why do you call me, 'Lord, Lord,' and do not do what
I say?*

Have you ever heard a story or an illustration that just sticks with you? I have, and it came from a television show called "How I Met Your Mother." Ted, the main character on the show, is an architect. While struggling with life and work, Ted tells this story to another character.

"One day, an architect was tasked with building a library. He worked hard and came up with a beautiful and eloquent design. When the project was finished, he was thrilled with the library, until the beautiful building began to sink into the foundation. While he designed a beautiful building, he had not considered the weight of all the books."

Ted then asked Robin, "What if I forget the weight of the books?" I think that is a question we need to ask ourselves after reading the parable Jesus told of the wise and foolish builders. When building the foundation of our lives, have we considered the storms that will come?

One thing we can't skip is the opening verse of the passage. Jesus asks, "Why do you call me Lord and don't do what I say?" The question is in the title and the authority we give to Jesus. If he is a good teacher, we can take what we like and leave the rest. We must follow everything he says if he is our Lord and King.

## Reflection Questions & Prayer

Currently, what is the foundation of your life built on?
Are you prepared for life's storms?
How are you responding to Jesus' teachings and instructions for your life?

## A.C.T.S. Prayer

# SCRIPTURE STUDY

## Luke 14:15-24

Read through the passage above and use the questions
below to help you dive deeper into God's word

---

**1**

**What did you observe in the passage?**
**What did I see?**
**What was the author saying?**

---

**2**

**What does the author mean by what he is saying?**
**What truth rises out of the text?**

---

**3**

**How Do I apply the truth from God's word?**

# INVITATION
# DECLINED

*Scripture: Luke 14:15-24*

*Luke 14:15*
*When one of those at the table with him heard this,*
*he said to Jesus, "Blessed is the one who will eat at the*
*feast in the kingdom of God."*

One of the coolest traditions in American sports is the invitation to the White House for teams that win a championship. The person holding the highest office in America invites the team to celebrate. I don't know what happens at one of these events, but I know the team gets their picture taken with the President. They gain access to a person and a place that most people never experience.

In the culture and political climate we live into day, acceptance or denial of the invite is a polarizing piece of news. If teams or players accept or decline the invite, it is discussed on both sides of the political aisle on social media outlets and news networks. When writing this devotion, headlines were made by a star player declining the invitation due to having something previously scheduled. We may never know the real motivation behind the invitation being declined, but there is no guarantee that the invitation will come around again.

In our study of Jesus' parables today, he uses the example of a master giving a banquet to teach another heavenly lesson. When we look at the parable, we can see ourselves in one of two places. The first is the people who were invited but declined for different reasons. None of the reasons was worth declining the master's invitation. Yet they still passed on a once-in-a- lifetime invite.

The second place we can see ourselves in this parable is the servant going out and offering the invitation. This is one of our primary roles as followers of Jesus. The servant would have known how great the master's house was. This helps us share the invitation because we know that this invitation is one you do not want to miss out on because the invitation of Jesus is an invitation to eternal life through him.

## Reflection Questions & Prayer

What material things in your life are causing you to say no to God?
What occupational things are causing you to say no to God?
What relationships are causing you to say no to God?

## A.C.T.S. Prayer

# SCRIPTURE STUDY
## Luke 6:46-49

Read through the passage above and use the questions
below to help you dive deeper into God's word

| ① | **What did you observe in the passage?**<br>**What did I see?**<br>**What was the author saying?** |
|---|---|
| | |

| ② | **What does the author mean by what he is saying?**<br>**What truth rises out of the text?** |
|---|---|
| | |

| ③ | **How Do I apply the truth from God's word?** |
|---|---|
| | |

# GROWTH, TRANSFORMATION & SEPERATION

*Scripture: Matthew 13:24-43*

*Matthew 13:43*
*Then the righteous will shine like the sun in the kingdom of their*
*Father. Whoever has ears, let them hear.*

While riding in the car the other day, my wife scrolled through old pictures on her phone. Pictures of our kids as babies and toddlers were coming up. It was a nice moment to look back and see the growth and transformation our kids have gone through over the years.

It also brought back memories of prayers we had prayed for our children. I can't count how many days and nights we spent praying over things out of our control—the memories of the prayers in the past led to praise of God in the present. The growth and transformation in our children were a physical representation of answered prayers.

Three things from today's study of Jesus' parables stand out to me. The first two are growth and transformation. While this parable is being used to give examples of what the kingdom of heaven is like, the gospel has the same effect on our lives. Our journey of following Jesus starts with one step, but the path is marked by growth and transformation.

The third thing I notice comes from the parable of the weeds. Everyone's journey here on earth ends with separation. The natural question to wonder is "how can I know if I am part of the wheat or the weeds"? Luckily for us, the bible helps us answer that question. First, have you accepted Jesus as your savior and Lord? That answer must be a yes to not be a part of the weeds. The second is, do you see growth and transformation in your life since you made that decision? Remember this side of heaven is about progress, not perfection.

## Reflection Questions & Prayer

What areas of your life can you see growth and transformation after accepting Jesus' offer of salvation?
What areas of your life do you need to ask God to help you work on?
How does knowing the world ends with separation affect how you look at sharing the gospel?

## A.C.T.S. Prayer

# SCRIPTURE STUDY

# Matthew 13:24-43

Read through the passage above and use the questions below
to help you dive deeper into God's word

**1**      **What did you observe in the passage?**
**What did I see?**
**What was the author saying?**

**2**      **What does the author mean by what he is saying?**
**What truth rises out of the text?**

**3**      **How Do I apply the truth from God's word?**

# THE JUICE IS WORTH THE SQUEEZE

*Scripture: Matthew 13: 1-23 & 44-46*

*Matthew 13:23*
*But the seed falling on good soil refers to someone*
*who hears the word and understands it. This is the*
*one who produces a crop, yielding a hundred, sixty or*
*thirty times what was sown."*

While coaching football in high school, I have a few stories that stick out. One such story is when we had an athlete break his hand for punching another player. The problem was that the other player was wearing a helmet at the time. I can't say for sure, but it's a safe bet that it happens to someone every football season. I remember this because of what another coach told him. He calmly told the player who broke his hand, "play stupid games, win stupid prizes".

The athlete did not consider what his actions would cost him. While the player he hit might have had a headache to deal with for a short time, his result was two to four weeks in a cast. It is safe to say that the juice was not worth the squeeze.

In our two parables today, Jesus first discusses seeds and crops. While three of the four ended with no crops, the one that fell on good soil yielded unbelievable amounts of fruit. The seed is the gospel, and when we make sure it falls on good ground, we see the fruit of God in our lives.

The second parable shows us that having Jesus in our lives is worth everything. In two different scenarios, we see someone give everything for what they find. They counted the cost, and all they had was worth giving for what they found. Following Jesus is not easy, but the juice is worth the squeeze.

## Reflection Questions & Prayer

What soil is the gospel falling on in your life?
If fruit is evidence of a healthy tree, what spiritual fruit do you see in your life? (Check out Galatians 5 to see the fruit of the Spirit)
If all God ever gave you was life in Jesus, would that be enough to give all you have for him? Or would you need more?

## A.C.T.S. Prayer

# SCRIPTURE STUDY

# Matthew 13:1-23 & 44-46

Read through the passage above and use the questions
below to help you dive deeper into God's word

---

**1**

**What did you observe in the passage?**
**What did I see?**
**What was the author saying?**

---

**2**

**What does the author mean by what he is saying?**
**What truth rises out of the text?**

---

**3**

**How Do I apply the truth from God's word?**

# COMMISSIONED

Week 4

DAVID PLATT

# THE GREAT COMMISSION WAS CLEARLY AND DEFINITELY NOT A CALL TO SIT BACK AND STAY SILENT IN A WORLD OF EVIL AND SIN AND SUFFERING. IT WAS A CALL TO STAND UP AND SPEAK CLEARLY

**Matthew 28:18-20** "_Therefore go and make disciples of all nations, baptizing them in the name of the Father and of the Son and of the Holy Spirit, 20 and teaching them to obey everything I have commanded you. And surely I am with you always, to the very end of the age._"

I have always been a history nerd. When I was little, I remember watching the History Channel with my granddad. I believe that drew me to the history of the military and its culture. God took that interest and used it not only to help my family during a rough season but also to give me a platform to share the gospel in my first book, Tier One Christianity. It is easy to look back now and see that God was shaping and preparing me to share the gospel in a specific way.

Out of my military interest, I developed a strong respect and admiration for the different military academies in America. The young men and women attending these institutions are some of the best and brightest our nation has to offer. They trade a traditional college experience for leadership training and opportunities they could not receive at any other college or university. At the end of their four years at the academy, they will walk away as commissioned officers in their respective branches of the military.

The commissioning gives them the right to lead and command those under them to accomplish the mission they are given. As followers of Jesus, we are also commissioned with a mission to undertake. The more we are cultivated in Jesus' teaching, the better we are prepared to take on Jesus' mission. The mission is broken down into three parts. The first is what (go and make disciples). The second is how (teaching them to obey all I have commanded you). Finally, the third is the support (I will be with you to the end of the age).

The last part of this study will be looking at how Jesus told us to live. While there are personal benefits to living that way, there are also benefits to the mission Jesus gave us. When you live differently from the world, people will naturally want to know why you are different. This gives us the platform to share why we are different, is we have the hope of glory, which is Christ in us! That is the good news we are given to share.

# Matthew 28

After the Sabbath, at dawn on the first day of the week, Mary Magdalene and the other Mary went to look at the tomb.

2 There was a violent earthquake, for an angel of the Lord came down from heaven and, going to the tomb, rolled back the stone and sat on it. 3 His appearance was like lightning, and his clothes were white as snow. 4 The guards were so afraid of him that they shook and became like dead men.

5 The angel said to the women, "Do not be afraid, for I know that you are looking for Jesus, who was crucified. 6 He is not here; he has risen, just as he said. Come and see the place where he lay. 7 Then go quickly and tell his disciples: 'He has risen from the dead and is going ahead of you into Galilee. There you will see him.' Now I have told you."

8 So the women hurried away from the tomb, afraid yet filled with joy, and ran to tell his disciples. 9 Suddenly Jesus met them. "Greetings," he said. They came to him, clasped his feet and worshiped him. 10 Then Jesus said to them, "Do not be afraid. Go and tell my brothers to go to Galilee; there they will see me."

11 While the women were on their way, some of the guards went into the city and reported to the chief priests everything that had happened. 12 When the chief priests had met with the elders and devised a plan, they gave the soldiers a large sum of money, 13 telling them, "You are to say, 'His disciples came during the night and stole him away while we were asleep.' 14 If this report gets to the governor, we will satisfy him and keep you out of trouble." 15 So the soldiers took the money and did as they were instructed. And this story has been widely circulated among the Jews to this very day.

16 Then the eleven disciples went to Galilee, to the mountain where Jesus had told them to go. 17 When they saw him, they worshiped him; but some doubted. 18 Then Jesus came to them and said, "All authority in heaven and on earth has been given to me. 19 Therefore go and make disciples of all nations, baptizing them in the name of the Father and of the Son and of the Holy Spirit, 20 and teaching them to obey everything I have commanded you. And surely I am with you always, to the very end of the age."

# GROUP DISCUSSION:

After reading through Matthew 28 discuss the following questions in your group

How does knowing Jesus is risen from the grave help you to face your fears?

Jesus says, "All authority in heaven and on earth has been given to me." How does that truth strengthen your trust in Him—especially when you're unsure, struggling, or sharing your faith?

Has there been a time when you stepped out to share your faith, encourage someone spiritually, or walk with someone in discipleship? What happened, and what did it show you about Jesus?

What does it mean to "go and make disciples" in your daily context—at school, work, or in your community?

Jesus promises, "I am with you always." How have you experienced His presence in real, personal ways? How has that become part of your testimony?

## WEEK 4

**MEMORY VERSE**

ACTS 1:8 BUT YOU WILL RECEIVE POWER WHEN THE HOLY SPIRIT COMES ON YOU; AND YOU WILL BE MY WITNESSES IN JERUSALEM, AND IN ALL JUDEA AND SAMARIA, AND TO THE ENDS OF THE EARTH.

MONDAY

TUESDAY

WEDNESDAY

**ACCOUNTABILITY PARTNER**_____

THURSDAY

FRIDAY

SATURDAY

SUNDAY

# DAILY DEVOTIONS

## WEEK 4

———

# COMMISSIONED

———

"THE GREAT COMMISSION IS
NOT AN OPTION TO BE
CONSIDERED; IT IS A COMMAND
TO BE OBEYED."
HUDSON TAYLOR

# POSITIVE PURPOSE

*Scripture: Matthew 5:13-16*

**Matthew 5:16**
*In the same way, let your light shine before others,*
*that they may see your good deeds and glorify your*
*Father in heaven.*

One question I have heard a lot during my life and have even asked multiple times myself is, "What does God want me to do with my life?" That question can simply be phrased like "How can I make a positive impact for Jesus?" It would be nice if God would give us a billboard with clear, step-by-step instructions on how to live the life God wants us to live. Unfortunately, that will likely not happen for you or me. While we may not get a billboard, we do, however, have instructions straight from the mouth of Jesus on our purpose for our lives.

The first part of living out God's commission is understanding our purpose. We find this in Matthew chapter five. There, Jesus tells the listeners they are the salt of the earth and the light of the world. It is in those words that we find our purpose: Be salt and be light.

This does not contradict the Great Commission in Matthew 28. Instead, it supports it. Jesus calls us to be the salt of the earth. Salt is a preservative that helps keep things. In a world flawed by morality, we must preserve and live the way God intended us to. We also know that because of sin, the world is in darkness. We also know that Jesus is the light of the world. So when we have Jesus, we have the light the world needs.

Being the salt of the earth and the light of the world will cause us to look different from the rest of the world. This will naturally bring up a question from non-believers of why you live the way you do. This is our opportunity to share Jesus and make disciples by sharing the thing that changes us...the gospel!

## Reflection Questions & Prayer

How does living the way Jesus called us to live positively impact morality?
Why is it important to show the light of Jesus to the world?
What areas of your life do you need to give to God to help you improve in?

## A.C.T.S. Prayer

# SCRIPTURE STUDY
# Matthew 5:13-16

Read through the passage above and use the questions
below to help you dive deeper into God's word

| 1 | **What did you observe in the passage?**<br>**What did I see?**<br>**What was the author saying?** |
|---|---|
|   |   |

| 2 | **What does the author mean by what he is saying?**<br>**What truth rises out of the text?** |
|---|---|
|   |   |

| 3 | **How Do I apply the truth from God's word?** |
|---|---|
|   |   |

# HATE IS HEAVY

*Scripture: Matthew 5:21-26*

*Matthew 5:23-24*
*23 "Therefore, if you are offering your gift at the altar and there remember that your brother or sister has something against you, 24 leave your gift there in front of the altar. First go and be reconciled to them; then come and offer your gift.*

The hardest thing I have ever done physically is a workout called Murph. During my late twenties, I started going to a CrossFit gym. One of the staples of CrossFit is hero workouts. They are physically demanding workouts that are given the names of different heroes. Murph is my favorite of the hero workouts because Lt. Michael Murphy is a personal hero of mine.

If you are unfamiliar with the " Murph" workout, let me try to paint you a picture of the pain I willingly put myself through. The first requirement is to wear a twenty-pound weight vest the entire time. To open the workout, you run a mile. Then you complete 100pull-ups, 200 push-ups, 300 air squats, and then you end the workout by running a mile. One year, when I attempted the workout, I tried to go as hard and fast as possible. My prize was a sense of pride and the feeling that I would die for three days. The workout is hard enough without the weight vest, but the extra weight takes it to a different level.

During a hard season, I felt like I was wearing a weight vest that I could not take off. I am ashamed to admit it, but the weight came from the hate I had for people who I thought had done me and my family wrong. That weight made everyday life hard and stole joy for longer than I care to admit.

Jesus tells us that if you hate someone in your heart, it's like committing murder. While the world encourages you to hate others who are different from you or oppose you, our savior teaches us the opposite. Part of our commissioning to live differently is a call to take off the weight of hate in your heart. Seek forgiveness from others and give forgiveness to those who sin against you. Life is better lived free from the weight of hate.

## Reflection Questions & Prayer

Are you carrying around hate in your heart for someone?
Do you need to ask for forgiveness from someone?
Is there someone you need to forgive?

**A.C.T.S. Prayer**

# SCRIPTURE STUDY

# Matthew 5:21-26

Read through the passage above and use the questions
below to help you dive deeper into God's word

| 1 | **What did you observe in the passage?**<br>**What did I see?**<br>**What was the author saying?** |
|---|---|
| | |

| 2 | **What does the author mean by what he is saying?**<br>**What truth rises out of the text?** |
|---|---|
| | |

| 3 | **How Do I apply the truth from God's word?** |
|---|---|
| | |

# GUARD YOUR HEART

*Scripture: Matthew 5:27-32*

*Matthew 5:27-28*
*27 "You have heard that it was said, 'You shall not commit adultery.' 28 But I tell you that anyone who looks at a woman lustfully has already committed adultery with her in his heart*

Protection is essential for valuable things. People will do different things to protect their possessions. This can range from a safe in their closet to a 24/7 security detail for the crown jewels of England. The value of what they want to protect influences how much they spend on security. Some people go to extremes to protect their possessions.

I read about one celebrity who had a moat installed around his home. While another celebrity bought an armored car like they use for the President of the United States. Protection does not just stop at extreme measures. In 2025, cars will come with features to keep you safe while driving. They range from heads-up driving displays to hands-free driving. Some cars even come with auto-correct, so if you start drifting into another lane or off the road, it corrects the car's path.

While we will go to extremes to protect our material possessions and ensure our safety while driving, we can be cavalier and careless regarding our hearts. We can offer our hearts to anyone who shows us attention or treats physical intimacy as if it is nothing more than a handshake. The truth is, the world does not encourage us to guard our hearts.

Jesus, however, does tell us to guard our hearts. While the physical act of adultery is easy to condemn, Jesus tells us that lust in the heart is the same as the physical act. It is no accident that Jesus discusses adultery and divorce back-to-back. Both actions don't just happen. By guarding our hearts, even when we are single, we can help keep ourselves from walking down that path.

## Reflection Questions & Prayer

Are you being careful or cavalier with your heart?
In what areas can you improve the protection of your heart?
Why is it problematic to give your heart to someone else before you give it to God?

### A.C.T.S. Prayer

# SCRIPTURE STUDY

# Matthew 5:27-32

Read through the passage above and use the questions
below to help you dive deeper into God's word

**1**

**What did you observe in the passage?**
**What did I see?**
**What was the author saying?**

**2**

**What does the author mean by what he is saying?**
**What truth rises out of the text?**

**3**

**How Do I apply the truth from God's word?**

# DISCIPLINE = FREEDOM

*Scripture: Matthew 6:1-18*

**Matthew 6:1**
*Be careful not to practice your righteousness in front
of others to be seen by them. If you do, you will have
no reward from your Father in heaven.*

Retired Navy SEAL Jocko Willink has a lot of titles, but the ones that stand out to me are teacher and motivator. Jocks uses the principles and lessons learned from years of combat experience to help people with everyday leadership and life. His book Discipline Equals Freedom: Field Manual is a personal favorite of mine. Jocko explained what that phrase means in an article for Forbes magazine in 2017. Jock was asked what the connection was between discipline and freedom. Jocko said, "While Discipline and Freedom seem like they sit on opposite sides of the spectrum, they are actually very connected. Freedom is what everyone wants — to be able to act and live with freedom. But the only way to get to a place of freedom is through discipline. If you want financial freedom, you have to have financial discipline. If you want more free time, you have to follow a more disciplined time management system.".

We all want the freedom to be able to live the life we want. Jocko's way of thinking is a way to achieve that goal. As followers of Christ, we want and desire that same thing. However, we are like Paul when he said in Romans 7:15, "I do not understand what I do. For what I want to do I do not do, but what I hate I do. "On this side of heaven, the desires of our flesh are not going away. So, how can we find spiritual freedom in a sinful world?

In the first part of Matthew 6, Jesus suggests three spiritual disciplines for his followers to practice. Notice how prayer, fasting, and giving are not suggested activities. He did not say "if you" do these things; he said "when you" do these things. Then, he tells us how those things should be done. Leaders give orders; great leaders explain how the order should be carried out. Thank God we have the most excellent leader ever!

## Reflection Questions & Prayer

How is your prayer life?
Are you listening to God or the world more?
Is your giving out of gratitude or requirement?
When was the last time you abstained from something for a period to focus on God?

### A.C.T.S. Prayer

# SCRIPTURE STUDY

# Matthew 6:1-18

Read through the passage above and use the questions
below to help you dive deeper into God's word

**1** **What did you observe in the passage?**
**What did I see?**
**What was the author saying?**

**2** **What does the author mean by what he is saying?**
**What truth rises out of the text?**

**3** **How Do I apply the truth from God's word?**

# WHIRWIND OF WORRY

*Scripture: Matthew 6:19-34*

*Matthew 6:21*
*For where your treasure is, there your heart will be also.*

Sometimes, events or seasons in life can cause you to feel like you're spinning. I have lived through a season like that from late 2021 through most of 2022. Looking back now, the spin I felt was not caused by what I was going through but by the worry and stress I added to the mix. The more I worried, the more my anxiety went from awhirl wind to a full-blown tornado. While I know you can't fight the wind, I tried and failed miserably during that season.

Knowing and doing are two completely different actions. We can know something is bad for us, yet we still do it. I knew worrying about the situation was not what God wanted me to do, but I did it anyway. Knowledge is not worth much if you don't put it into practice.

The problem I ran into was finding something to replace the worry with. Projects are great and can be positive additions to the world, but you can't work on a project 24/7. No matter what creates the void, things will always try to fill it. Worry and anxiety are great at finding the empty spaces of your life and filling them with all the fear and anguish they can squeeze into the gap.

While there is no cure for keeping worry and anxiety from ever creeping into your life, there is a great weapon we have as followers of Jesus to combat them: worship. I heard a pastor say you can't worry and worship at the same time. There is never a moment when Jesus is not worthy of all the praise we can bring him. By moving from worry to worship, you take the focus off you and focus on how great, loving, powerful, faithful, and dependable God is. The more you know about him, the more fuel you have for your worship.

## Reflection Questions & Prayer

Is your focus on earthly or heavenly treasure?
When was the last time you worshiped with all of your heart?
Have you gone to God with the causes of your worry and anxiety?

## A.C.T.S. Prayer

# SCRIPTURE STUDY

# Matthew 6:19-34

Read through the passage above and use the questions
below to help you dive deeper into God's word

**1** | **What did you observe in the passage?**
**What did I see?**
**What was the author saying?**

**2** | **What does the author mean by what he is saying?**
**What truth rises out of the text?**

**3** | **How Do I apply the truth from God's word?**

# THE JAIL CELL OF BEING JUDGMENTAL

*Scripture: Matthew 7*

**Matthew 7:2**
*For in the same way you judge others, you will be judged, and
with the measure you use, it will be measured to you.*

I have been blessed with opportunities to visit correctional facilities (jails) and share the gospel with the men there. While only going a few times, I have learned a few things. The first is that prisons are a mission field that needs people to go and share the good news of Jesus with the men and women who live there. The second is that I don't mind visiting for a few hours, but don't want to live there. I don't know anyone who would willingly choose incarceration over freedom.

Yet, strangely enough, many people choose to live in metaphorical jail cells because of their judgmental attitudes without realizing it. By passing judgment on others, we are trying to escape the guilt we feel from our own sins. It may sound like this in your head:" I know I am not perfect, but what I did was not as bad as what they did." The judgment of others does not place us on a higher moral platform; it buries us deeper in our self-incarceration.

In Matthew 7, Jesus says that before we look at the sins of others, we must first examine ourselves. We do that by looking at God's holiness. When we do that, we see that we don't compare and we never will. That takes us back to the cross and the gift of God's grace which leads to repentance and freedom that is only found in Jesus.

Only after we repent of our sin can we clearly see how to help others. It is a paradigm shift in looking at others' sins. From looking at it and passing judgment to make ourselves feel better. To the realization, you need to point that person to the cross to find love, grace, and freedom. The bible does not tell us that the wages of our sin is moral inferiority. It tells us the wages of our sin is death. Our job is to point people to the life and freedom we have found in Jesus.

## Reflection Questions & Prayer

Do you use the actions of other to place yourself on the moral high ground to feel better about yourself?
Has judging the sin of someone else ever brought you closer to God?
What sin do you need to repent of today?

A.C.T.S Prayer

# SCRIPTURE STUDY

# Matthew 7

Read through the passage above and use the questions
below to help you dive deeper into God's word

**1** **What did you observe in the passage?**
**What did I see?**
**What was the author saying?**

**2** **What does the author mean by what he is saying?**
**What truth rises out of the text?**

**3** **How Do I apply the truth from God's word?**

# TREASURE MAP

### Scripture: Matthew 5:1-12

### Matthew 5:3
*"Blessed are the poor in spirit,*
*for theirs is the kingdom of heaven*

In 1985, the world received a gift in the form of a cinematic masterpiece known as "The Goonies". This marvelous tale tells of kids searching for the treasure of One-Eyed Willy to save their homes from being bought and having to move. The possibility of a life-changing discovery propelled them on the journey. The knowledge that there was no tomorrow gave them the resolve to keep going. While we all like to think we are the ones searching for the treasure, as followers of Jesus, we are the map for the rest of the world.

Jesus said in John 10:10, "The thief comes only to steal and kill and destroy; I have come that they may have life, and have it to the full". People search for life, and the world points them in the wrong direction. As followers of Jesus, we know that life is only found in Christ. While God has and can speak to people in different ways, we are blessed to be part of his mission today. How can my life be a map to life in Jesus?

The Greek word for blessed in Matthew chapter 5 is "Makarios". It means receiving God's favor or being in a position of favor. However, the beatitudes found in Matthew 5 are not steps to complete to be blessed; they are steps to take out of the blessing of knowing Jesus and being made right with God. By living out the beatitudes, we will be able to point people to the source of our blessing, Jesus, and by doing that, we are completing his great commission: to know him and to make him known to the world.

### Reflection Questions & Prayer

Do you believe that Jesus is the greatest treasure we could find?
Do you believe it is worth losing everything else for?
Are you living your life as a map pointing people to Jesus?

### A.C.T.S. Prayer

# SCRIPTURE STUDY

# Matthew 5:1-12

Read through the passage above and use the questions
below to help you dive deeper into God's word

| ① | What did you observe in the passage?<br>What did I see?<br>What was the author saying? |
|---|---|
| | |

| ② | What does the author mean by what he is saying?<br>What truth rises out of the text? |
|---|---|
| | |

| ③ | How Do I apply the truth from God's word? |
|---|---|
| | |

# NEXT STEPS

# MARATHON NOT A SPRINT

*1ˢᵗ John 2:5-6*

*₅ But if anyone obeys his word, love for God is truly made complete in them. This is how we know we are in him: ₆ Whoever claims to live in him must live as Jesus did.*

Have you ever been hooked on a show and you binge all the episodes as fast as you can? I know that has been my story multiple times in my life. The common thing I find after the final episode is a sense of emptiness in my life. Something that I have dedicated so much time to leaves a void when it comes to an end. The question is, what do I feel that gap with now?

Thank you for creating time and space over the last 28 days to become more captivated and cultivated in the life and teaching of Jesus, as well as understanding the commission He gave you as one of His followers. I hope and pray that all of those things were accomplished during our time together. The excellent news for you is that even though this study is over, there does not have to be avoid in your life!

During the time of this study, we have only scratched the surface of the greatness, wonder, and awe that can be experienced in a relationship with Jesus. The author of Hebrews tells us in chapter 4 that "the word of God is alive and active." While there may not be a day 29 devotion for you, there is a living love letter from God to you that you have access to daily. Hopefully, over the last few weeks, you have developed the daily habit of spending time in God's Word.

Following Jesus is like running a marathon compared to a sprint. It's about stamina, and to build that takes putting in the work over and over again. Over the past few weeks, you have established a solid foundation, but you still need to put in daily effort. The work is not so that God will love us, but it is because God loves us!

So, look for other devotionals or bible reading plans and start them tomorrow. Find an app that you like. Whatever you do, just keep growing in your relationship. When you do, you will be amazed at how awesome it is that you get to know the King of kings on a personal level, and get to be a part of accomplishing his mission!

God Bless & Stay In Your 3 Foot World
Drew

# RESOURCES

# GROUP LEADER GUIDE

## Role Of The Leader

If you lead a group through this study, thank you for investing in others' walk with Jesus. Here are a few things that can help you out. The first is to remember that you are not a professor giving a lecture; you are a guide who points the group to Jesus. Secondly, lead by example by being vulnerable with the group and encouraging conversation. Never be scared to stop studying and pray for someone in the group, or have the group pray for you. Finally, try to create an atmosphere that is inviting to nonbelievers and seasoned Christians.

## Tips for Group Discussion

Failure to plan is planning to fail. This is an excellent motto for anyone leading a project, but it is especially great for approaching this study. Please feel free to share your thoughts on every question. It also helps to have other questions that stem from the main one. Make sure to give people time to process the question. Sometimes, silence is not a bad thing. Above all else, always point people to Jesus and what the Bible says about issues or topics.

## Sample Group Session Format

**Welcome: (5-10 min)** Greet everyone, introduce new folks, and use a fun or meaningful question to get people talking. Example: "What was your high/low this week?" or "What's your favorite worship song and why?"

**Bible Study and discussion: (30-45 min)** Read the bible passage and walk through the discussion questions

**Personal Sharing ( 10-15 min):** Invite group members to share some things that stood out to them from daily devotions from the week. This is also a great time to share Jesus' Stories. Jesus' stories are stories from the week where they got to see or be a part of what god is doing.

**Accountability and Prayer (10-15 min):** Check in on your swim buddy, or receive a swim buddy for the week. Share prayer needs and take time to pray for others for the upcoming week.

# GROUP LEADER GUIDE

## Leading With Confidence Tips

- Start with prayer. Ask the Spirit to lead you each week — before, during, and after your group.

- Facilitate, don't dominate. Guide the conversation, but let others share. Silence is okay!

- Create safety. Set a tone of respect: no interrupting, no shaming, everything shared stays private.

- Celebrate progress. Even small steps in Scripture memory, prayer, or vulnerability matter!

- Follow up midweek. Send a text of encouragement or check in with group members.

# PRAYER REQUEST

# PRAYER REQUEST

# PRAYER REQUEST

# PRAYER REQUEST

# Sermon
## Notes

**Sermon Topic**

**Pastor**

**Date**

**Date:**

### SCRIPTURE

### DETAILS

### APPLICATION

### SUMMARY

# Sermon
## Notes

**Sermon Topic**

**Pastor**

**Date**

**Date:**

### S C R I P T U R E

### D E T A I L S

### A P P L I C A T I O N

### S U M M A R Y

# Sermon
## Notes

**Sermon Topic**

**Pastor**

**Date**

**Date:**

### SCRIPTURE

_____
_____
_____
_____
_____
_____
_____
_____
_____
_____
_____

### DETAILS

_____
_____
_____
_____
_____
_____
_____
_____
_____
_____
_____

### APPLICATION

_____
_____
_____
_____
_____
_____
_____
_____
_____
_____
_____

### SUMMARY

_____
_____
_____
_____
_____
_____
_____
_____
_____
_____
_____

# Sermon
## Notes

**Sermon Topic**

**Pastor**

**Date**

**Date:**

### SCRIPTURE

_____
_____
_____
_____
_____
_____
_____
_____
_____
_____
_____

### DETAILS

_____
_____
_____
_____
_____
_____
_____
_____
_____
_____
_____

### APPLICATION

_____
_____
_____
_____
_____
_____
_____
_____
_____
_____

### SUMMARY

_____
_____
_____
_____
_____
_____
_____
_____
_____
_____

# Other Projects by Drew Alan Hall

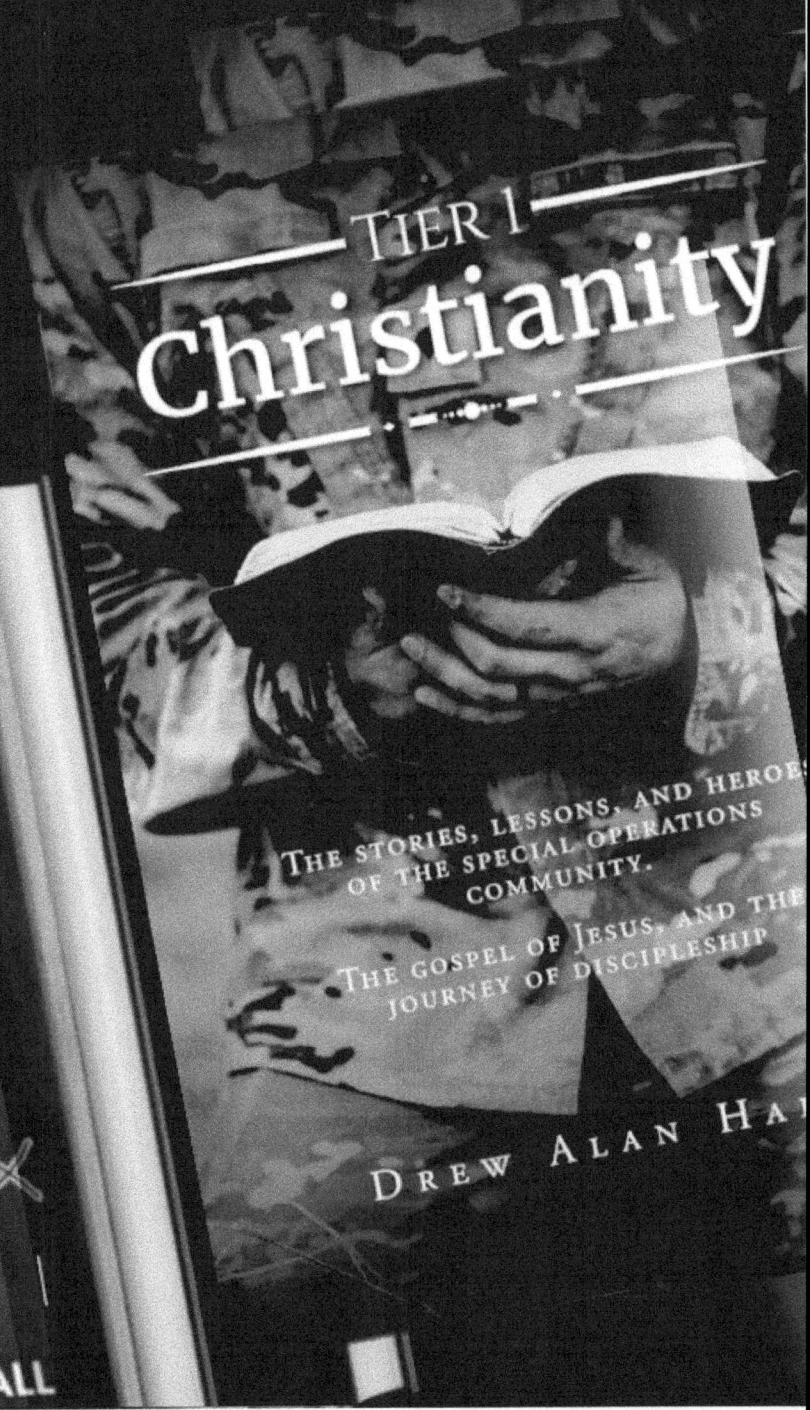

# ABOUT KHARIS PUBLISHING:

Kharis Publishing, an imprint of Kharis Media LLC, is a leading Christian and inspirational book publisher based in Aurora, Chicago metropolitan area, Illinois. Kharis' dual mission is to give voice to under-represented writers (including women and first-time authors) and equip orphans in developing countries with literacy tools. That is why, for each book sold, the publisher channels some of the proceeds into providing books and computers for orphanages in developing countries so that these kids may learn to read, dream, and grow. For a limited time, Kharis Publishing is accepting unsolicited queries for nonfiction (Christian, self-help, memoirs, business, health and wellness) from qualified leaders, professionals, pastors, and ministers. Learn more at: https://kharispublishing.com/

# PRAISE FOR CAPTIVATED, CULTIVATED, COMMISSIONED

---

Doing this study has truly changed my life. The reflective questions at the end of each day made me dig way deeper into the meaning of what God really wanted me to grasp. I found that the topics were something that I really needed to hear and allowed me to apply that new knowledge to my everyday life. If you are someone who struggles to read the Bible every day, I really recommend this study to help you get hungry for God's word!
—Shannon Weems, Samford Softball

This bible study has allowed me to actually grow in my faith. It showed me that even with a busy schedule, there is time for God. It also helped show me how much the Lord truly loves us. It also helped apply it directly to my life, as the stories are so relatable to everyday life. I have never felt closer to God than I have with this study!
—Joi Hubbard, Samford Softball

"This Bible study got me excited to get into God's word again! I often struggle with where to start when reading my Bible, but this study walked me through the teachings of Jesus in a deeper way. The devotionals allowed me to connect with the scriptures, and the reflection questions allowed me to apply what I was learning to my own life!"
—Olivia Trout, Samford Softball